Moments of a Lifetime December 10th '09

Mrs. Barry,
　　I hope my book is as ~~speaci~~ oops! special to you as the time we had together in gr. 2 is to me!

　　Lesley ♥ Butler

Moments of a Lifetime

A Collection of Writing

Lesley Butler

Copyright © 2009 by Lesley Butler.

ISBN: Softcover   978-1-4363-7959-5

All rights reserved. No part of this book may be reproduced or transmitted in any form or by any means, electronic or mechanical, including photocopying, recording, or by any information storage and retrieval system, without permission in writing from the copyright owner.

This book was printed in the United States of America.

To order additional copies of this book, contact:
Xlibris Corporation
1-888-795-4274
www.Xlibris.com
Orders@Xlibris.com

Contents

LOVE
Some Days 3
I Just Needed You 5
To Have and To Hold 7
Hate . . . ? 8
The Day My Heart Broke 9
The Impact of Love 10

ANGER & PAIN
Anger 17
Pain & Hurt 20
The Need To Heal 22
Hope 24

DEPRESSION
A Young Girl Cries in the Middle of the Night 27
Change 29
Sickness 31
Realization 32
The Truth About Depression 33

LIMITLESS FREEDOM
Can-Can 37
The Road 39
The Crossroad 41
A Deer Hunter's Prayer 43

HANDLING LIFE
Don't Worry, I'll be Fine 47
I'm Watching Over You 49
Heartache 50
Friends Forever 52
A Cancer Patient's Prayer 54

WAR
Good-Bye 59
I AM 60
I Pray 61
The Letter Home 62

YESTERDAY'S HISTORY
The R.M.S Titanic 67
The Imprisonment of High Society 70

To Amy & Paige,
Because without the two of you in my life,
I would have too few memorable moments.

A Special Thanks to:
Ms. Primeau
Mrs. Robertson
Caitlin Thorne
&
Wednesday Bell
For their help with editing.

A Special Thanks to:
Sheri Latchford
For her service in taking my photo.

~ *LOVE* ~

"Roses wither away,
Fires re-burn,
Tears dry,
Pain heals,
But True Love will never die"

Some Days

Some days
I love you.
All I want to do is hold you close.
I don't want to let you go,
I don't want to look down the line,
I just want to see us here and now,
Together.

Some days
I hate you.
I want to hit you,
I want to hit you harder than any other person could imagine.
Some days, the hate I feel for you is *almost*
Greater than the love I feel for you.
I want to push you away and never see you again.
Then . . .
I look into your eyes and
The anger and frustration seems to be washed away
As fast as it came ashore.
At that moment I forget why I even felt the hate that I did.

Some days
I hate you,
More than most.
I hate you more than just a stupid mistake that I made.
I want to push you farther,
And farther away.
Until you are only a dot on the horizon.

Some days
I want to scream,
Louder and louder,
For the whole world to hear.
I want them to know what you did.
I want them to hear me loud and clear.

Some days
I wonder if you know that I hate you.
I wonder if you realize the hurt you caused me.
I question if I should tell you anything about the hate.
Should you know about how you hurt me?
Should you know about the pain you cause me at times?
Would you even care?
Would you try to correct the mistake that you made?
Accident or not?
Then I wonder if you would care about the fact that,
Once I look into your eyes,
Life's little problems just melt away?

But most days . . . I love you.

I Just Needed You

Why did you do that to me?
Why did you hurt me?
Why would you say yes then not follow through?
You turned around and broke a promise.
That day I hated you more than anything.
I hated you more than light hates darkness.
I hated you more than the Devil hates God.
More than fire hates water.
I hated you.
I hated you more than ever at that moment you turned your back.

You hurt me.
I felt the pain,
More than you could imagine.
Part of me wanted to scream.
Another wanted to beat you.
One part wished I could fall to the ground and begin to cry.
I had no idea how to feel about you at that moment.

Should I
Have hated you?
Should I have forgave you and moved on?
Or should I have just pushed you over the edge,
In hopes to never see you again?
What was I to do?
You left me in the air,
And the world just seemed to stop.
The worst part was that you didn't even seem to care.
My heart and soul was in pain.
I tried to hide it,
But the hurt I felt could not be hidden even on the darkest of days.
Did you even see me there?
Did you even give a waking thought that I was in pain?

I said that I could forgive you,
But now . . .
I'm not so sure.
Should I forgive you?
Should I forgive and forget?
Should I just move on with my life still with the pain deep inside?
Or should I just move on without you?

Still,
I look at you and think,
Does he still care?
Does he *even* care?
You hurt me many times before,
But never like this time.
This time,
Will take longer than ever before for me to forgive.
I may forgive,
but I will never forget!
I will always remember,
The pain,
The hurt,
The tears,
I may have wanted to slap you.
I may have wanted to scream,
And I may have wanted to break down and cry,
But I really wanted to feel your arms around me.

I just wanted to feel loved.
I wanted to feel like you were by my side.
I wanted you there.
Right there, right then.
I wanted you.
Then I needed to forgive you.
I may have been in pain,
I may have been tearing myself apart inside,
And I may have been letting streams of tears fall to the ground,
But . . .
I needed to get past
the hurt,
the pain,
and the tears.
In the end . . .
I just needed you!

To Have and To Hold

I long to share a kiss with you.
To feel your lips against mine,
I long to feel your arms around me.
To share the love I feel for you.
Your warmth,
To keep me warm even on the coldest of days,

I long to feel your touch,
Your touch against mine,
And the love expressed by it.
I long to have you by my side,
Everyday.
I long to have my arms around you,
To hold you,
To kiss you,
To look into your eyes.
And see the man that you truly are.

Hate...?

I hate you,
I hate the way you walk,
I hate the way you look at me,
I hate the way you talk,
I hate the way you always see me,
Whether or not I'm looking for attention.
I hate your personality,
I hate your laugh,
I hate your voice,
That's all I ever hear around you.
I hate the time I spend with you.
I hate the way you make me laugh,
I hate the way you make me cry,
I hate the way you make me blush inside.
I hate your jokes,
I hate your looks,
I hate your smile,
I hate your glare,
I hate your stare,
But...
As you stare,
I stare back into your eyes.
That is when I realize what I love about you.

The Day My Heart Broke

The moment I heard that you were hers,
A fire within the very depths of my soul began to rage with the fury of a
thousand fires.
I had wanted to be with you for so long,
Then she took you out of sight in such a way that it reminded me of how
a hawk steels its
prey from a field
And I am the other hawk . . .
Starving . . . .

I looked her up and down,
I was crushed as I realized how much better she was than I.
Her hair gold as the sun and sits perfect to the viewing eye.
She has the figure of a doll with a touch as warm and gentle as a mother's.
Her eyes are what I truly despise.
They are as blue as a sapphire and as one looks into them you see the ocean.
When I,
however,
look into her eyes, I see the predators of the water swimming in circles,
Waiting for their next victim.

I take a step back to examine.
I watch for gaps between you and her.
It isn't until then that I realize that jealously is consuming my life.
I have lowered myself to her level.
As I close my eyes in shame,
I carefully run through the plans I have invented to slide between you
and her.

You are my true love and yet I have lost you,
To a thief that doesn't even know the crime she has committed.
My heart is dead and will be,
Until I feel that gentle touch of your skin.

The Impact of Love

I sat in the restaurant reflecting on everything that was going on in my life. Some things didn't seem like they happened and some seemed like they had such a huge impact on my life. As I thought more and more about all the emotions and problems that I had been experiencing for so long, I came to the conclusion that I was depressed. I wasn't like the usual person suffering from depression, I wasn't depressed about my life, I was depressed about how I was living it. I'd sit in a classroom day after day, and unwillingly listen to a passionless person ramble on and on about a subject that I had learned multiple times before. I could be out in the world doing something great with my life; I could be writing, singing, performing, or a star athlete. I feel as though I was wasting my life. I feel that each day I sat in a classroom counting the days until I could get out of this hell hole, I could be doing something useful with my life or at least tricking myself into thinking that I was doing something with my life.

As I lifted the cup of hot chocolate to my lips, I spied a young man over in the corner. He was reading a novel with a black cover and a gold ring on it. I realized he was reading one of Tolkien's amazing books that took so many people into the world of Middle-Earth. At first I didn't think he knew that I was watching him, until he pulled his eyes away from his book and glanced over at me. My heart sank as I looked into his handsome green eyes. His eyes were warm and greeting; his smile was bright enough to lighten any room on a gloomy day. I couldn't help but smile at him, he seemed so perfect at first glance.

He took the last bite of his bagel and rose from his seat. I was shocked and frozen stiff as he headed in my direction. I didn't want to talk to him, yet I desperately wanted to know his name. As he moved closer and closer, I examined his appearance a little more carefully. Blue jeans and a black zip up sweat shirt, it was a comfortable appearance, something like I'd wear. Today, however, was an exception. I was not wearing my usual comfortable clothing that I'd usually wear around the small village of St. Paul's. Instead I wore an expensive skirt with a white blouse, my hair was in a long elegant French braid. As I dolled myself up this morning, I thought that if I dressed up it would rid me of all the pain that was deep inside me. I thought that it would make me feel much better about myself. Like usual though, my assumptions were wrong! I felt more depressed as I wished I looked beautiful or at least what the media calls beautiful.

"Hello," he said as he placed his hands on the empty chair that sat on the other side of the table. I thought he was very forward as he just suddenly came up to me. I was somewhat suspecting and in some way hoping that he was on his way out, as my table sat next to the door.

"Do you mind if I sit down?" He asked, his voice scruffy. It reminded me of a farmer's voice, or at least the type of voice Hollywood wants us to believe that farmers have. I responded to his forward question with a nod.

When he sat down, we examined each other. To the eye we seemed so different. Somewhere inside I thought that we might be the same since I was known for being a very forward, blunt, and sometimes an arrogant person.

"Are you going to a wedding or something?" He asked, finally looking as though he was comfortable sitting at the table talking to me about the world, my appearance, and anything else that might cross his mind.

"No, I felt like I should dress up today." In a way, I was lying and in a way, I was telling the truth. I wanted to look good, but once I was dressed up, I second guessed myself about the whole thing.

"Well, either way, you look very nice." The word *nice* is not my favourite word for a couple reasons. One, *nice*, at one point in history, meant foolish. Two, anyone can do so much better than nice.

As I sipped my cup, I glanced out the window, and now that I think about it, I must have made him think that I wasn't interested.

"By the way I'm Al." He stuck his hand out at me with a friendly smile on his kissable lips.

"Anne," I replied, shaking his warm hand, that was it! That was the day that I was hit by what people call . . . "The Thunder Bolt." As I looked deep into his eyes, something inside clicked or broke. I'm not sure what happened, but we connected. Whether it was something clicking, or the wall I used to isolate myself from the world around me came crashing down, or just my heart beating so fast I had no idea what was going on; I was enlightened with a wave of happiness.

We sat at that table for hours on end, talking about everything under and beyond the sun. It was so perfect. I enjoyed talking to Al. I enjoyed listening to his opinions and why he thought the way he did. He was so different from any other man I had ever met. He listened to me, he made eye contact, and he didn't look away when I was talking about something that didn't interest him. He seemed so perfect, not only to my eyes, but now he seemed so perfect to my heart, my mind and my soul. He actually fit that perfect mold that I wished for so long would be filled.

As the restaurant came closer to closing time, we finished our conversation and walked out, leaving the waitresses to finish clearing the tables. Al walked me to my car, but I didn't want to leave. I wanted to talk to him forever.

Unfortunately, we arrived at my car. I reached into my pocket and pulled out my keys. I played with them for a couple seconds, waiting for him to say something, but he didn't.

"Well, it was nice talking to you." I reluctantly threw those words out as I unlocked the driver side door and slid in.

"Anne, I was wondering if you would like to meet again? Tomorrow, same place? Same time?" The way that Al asked the questions scared me, he asked it as though he knew I was going to say yes. His tone of voice was very low and deep, almost as if he only wanted me to hear him speak. Again I smiled, how could I not? I was attracted to him, why shouldn't I see "Perfect Fit" again?

That night was the longest night of my life, I was replaying all our conversations over and over in my head. I couldn't read, I couldn't watch T.V., and I couldn't keep my thoughts straight. It was like being drunk in a way. I was gitty, I was smiling from ear to ear, and nothing could take that smile away. For the first time in a long long time, I was happy. Truly happy. It wasn't until I gave into the thought of trying to go to sleep that I realized . . . he fixed it. I could look in the mirror and not turn away in misery, wishing I looked like someone else. When I thought about my overachieving sister that was a couple years older than I, I didn't feel pressured to have grades through the roof of my last year in college before I broke into the world. When I thought about all the stress and pressure my mom had thrown at me over the years, I didn't break into tears. Instead . . . I said, "Whatever." As I remembered all the times that I was assaulted and harassed, I didn't let it get the best of me. I stood tall with my chin high and vowed one more time and for the last time that I wasn't going to let it rule my life any longer.

It had happened eight years ago, and I still had the wound left wide open, without a band-aid, without a stitch, without anything to cover it, or at least to make it heal or come close to healing. For the first time in eight years that wound started to heal.

I read over my diary entires from that era in my life. I was reminded of how much closer I felt to God for giving me the strength to overcome an obstacle with which no one should ever have to deal. That was a horrific time in my life and as I read over my diary entries from that in my life. I tried to think of how I think of it now, at twenty-two years of age. I didn't forgive him, I just finally received the strength to move on with my life.

The next day, I was ecstatic! I couldn't wait to see Al again as I walked into the restaurant and sat at the exact same table. It wasn't long until he came through the door with a smile on his face as our eyes met. I took a deep breath.

"Good day sir." I said with a touch of sarcasm.

Again we sat at that table, talking for hours and hours. Nothing could have been more perfect. About half way through our *date,* I realized something so huge that my heart sank even deeper than it had the day before. He had changed my life. Those four words say so little for something so true. I glanced down at myself to check what exactly I had pulled out of my closet that morning before I met with Al. I was wearing something gorgeous, I was dressed as if I was going in for an interview for an important, life changing job and I hadn't tried to dress that way. I didn't wake up early and wish I could just drown myself in sleep. I didn't wake up and say, "I hate today!" I did something that was good for myself without having to put any thought into it. **He had changed my life.** I wanted to dress amazingly that day, I wanted to get up and see him. I had made so many breakthroughs the night before with my emotional-self that it *was* funny. As I listened to him talk, I couldn't decide whether or not I should tell him. I barely knew Al, but I felt like I knew everything there was to know about him.

As days turned into weeks, and weeks turned into months, Al and I had fallen in love. It was perfect, almost too perfect. I waited and waited for him to turn around and leave me behind in the dust. In the end . . . I was right. After we both graduated from college, Al received a job offer that was on the other side of the country. The day he asked me to go with him and I said no, my heart was ripped from my chest and stomped on. My life was in St. Paul's, I had grown up there and I had planned to live there until the last of my days. For once . . . Al couldn't see it my way and I couldn't see it his.

I watched him board the plane that day. Exactly a year and half to the day that we had met, Al was leaving me. I couldn't do anything but cry, he wanted the job and needed it, but I had to be the selfish one. As I got home, I cried for hours wondering if I would see him again. In the middle of the night I realized that if we were meant to be together, I would see him again and we would fall in love all over again.

Weeks passed and I wished I could just go after him, but I was working hard and I desperately needed the money. I couldn't just pack up and leave an important job up in the air. I really wanted to go after him and have our own Hollywood moment when we'd realized we're perfect for each other and he'd take me into his arms and kiss me. Too bad I was caught up in the romantic ideas of Hollywood.

I once heard the saying, "There are two tragedies in life. One, to lose your heart's desire and two, to gain your heart's desire." As I thought more and more about it I finally understood what it meant. I had lost my heart's desire, and yes, it was a tragedy. I had also gained my heart's desire a year and a half ago, and if I hadn't of met Al, I wouldn't have had to face the pain of losing him.

I went to that restaurant where we first met. I sat at that exact same table, wearing the exact same skirt and the exact same blouse, drinking hot chocolate. Once again I reflected on everything that was going on in my life. I was wasting time just waiting for Al to show up out of the blue, I could be doing something much more interesting with my life then wondering where I was going to be in the next year. I was almost in tears as the door swung open, breaking my concentration. It wasn't until I looked at the door that I realized it was all going to get better.

"Al?" I couldn't believe it, I was overflowing with joy. It was him, it was my life, my anti-depressant, my cure for the common problem.

"Anne, I love you." He announced his voice was the low and deep like it was on our first meeting.

"I love you too." I said the four words I had been longing to say. I jumped out of my seat and ran up to him. He took me into his arms, we gazed into each other's eyes as we leaned in closer. As our lips touched, we both realized that we were meant to be together.

~ ANGER & PAIN ~

"Anger and pain . . . both so powerful they have the ability to consume an entire life."

Anger

Anger clouded her mind,
The rage was like a fire in the pit of her stomach.
She would explode at the sight of that woman.
She had never been so enraged in her life,
The anger she felt . . .
Rage was even an understatement.
"How could one person make a fire burn so fierce?"

She tried to control it,
She tried and tried.
But she felt she was losing the battle between her and the fiery of rage
that boiled in a cauldron in the bottom of her soul.
She closed her eyes and tried to compose herself,
Even thoughts of weekends with friends did not lessen the painful fire
that burned
hotter and hotter by the second.

She finally gave in and stood on her own two feet.
She stomped out of the building,
Without thought, she began to run.
The stress powered her legs giving them the speed of a beast.
She couldn't control her anger,
why should she stay waiting to explode on some poor innocent victims?

She couldn't think straight as she ran farther and farther down the road.
The anger clouded her mind.
She stopped.
She dropped to her knees on the cool wet grass on the side of the road.
Tears began to fall,
She felt as though she was now hopeless and no one could help her.
Tricks of controlling her anger had been tried over and over . . .
None had worked.
The feeling of hopelessness made her believe that,
She must be a lost cause if she can not control
The anger,
The rage,
And the stress
that have formed in her heart and soul.

"How can I defeat a monster if I cannot even walk onto the battlefield?"
She cried
wiping the tears of depression from her face.
Is there anyway to defend against a monster that poses an almost
invincible threat?
She didn't wish to look at herself as she reminisced about all the other
times she had been so furious. She felt like a time bomb about to
explode within seconds.
Too many times had she felt that way,
Too many times did she feel there was no hope left in the world
to help her get through this rut in her life.
How could anyone get out of a rut that digs itself deeper and deeper
with everyday she sits in it?

She wiped the final tears that had fallen and sat up . . . still in pain.
"Where is the hope that I once had?" She questioned as she
saw the distance that she had ran to get away from her problems.
This was not the first time she had taken the chance of running,
Many had told her to just *cool down*,
How can she *cool down* and relax,
If it is almost impossible when she rests her head at night?
"Face your problems" was also another piece of advice given to her.
How can she face her problems if half the time she does not know what
they are.
She is told to keep her tongue tied and to not speak her mind.
"How can anyone face their problems if they are told not to speak up?"
She wonders.

As she watches the road, she sees a friend heading towards her.
As she sees her coming closer, she wonders if she should run even
farther away.
She decides not to as she is so close that the colour of her eyes can be seen
from where she sits on the side of the road.
Her friend doesn't talk at first, she only sits in silence as if waiting,
For her to speak up about her problems.
The moments of silence that sits between them seems like such a long
time.
Yet, it does not bother either of them.

Both wait for the other to speak, yet the friend does not choose to speak.

As they turn to each other, they both read each other's facial expressions.
Fear,
Anger,
Heartbreak,
Depression are easily read on her tear soaked face.
The friend is harder to read, she looks interested to help,
But she also looks content as she waits for words to be spoken that are not her's.
Still neither speak for a long time.
The friend looks deep into her eyes and sees the extent of the pain and hurt that are hidden from the world,
Slowly the blank expression sitting on her face turns to a smile of enlightenment.
"Maybe there is hope for me." She thinks smiling back at her angel.

Pain & Hurt

I never thought it was possible, but reality decided to prove me wrong,
I felt my heart split into pieces.
I felt the pain with every beat,
And the hurt as it cracked into millions of pieces.
I was in pain, my soul wondered what was happening.
It tried to find a way to save my heart before it was too late.
The blow hit the most tender part of my heart so fast and so fierce,
That I could not prepare for it.

At first I wasn't sure how to react,
Then as time began to unfold.
I began to realize how I should have reacted.
I sat in my seat staring out the window,
The world seemed to pass me by and I could not control it.
I felt as though I was watching my life through a pane of glass.

Slowly I let my mind wonder then I began to ponder.
I questioned why those words that I just heard had hurt me,
In a way that I had never been hurt before.
I began to think very deeply about it and slowly the prick that I had felt,
Turned into a heart wrenching pain that I could hardly bare.
My soul melted as the tears fell from my eyes like a heavy downpour.
My mind could not grasp the pain that I was feeling.
How could anyone hurt one person in such a way . . .
That she re-examines everything about her life and,
Everything that she thought could be?

I began to drift in and out of reality.
I was watching the world but I wasn't seeing anything.
My heart was pummeled,
No,
ripped from my chest and fed to a savage monster.
My soul had dissolved into a mass that I could not give a name.
There were no words to describe how I felt as I realized I could never
hold you in my arms.

Or feel your hand hold mine,
Or know that in your heart you feel the same as I.

No words could ever even understand the pain and hurt I put myself
through!
No words could understand why the tears that fell from my eyes had,
So much meaning to their existence.
I don't even think that I could ever understand why such simple words,
Could hurt my spirit so immensely.
No one will understand how I feel.
No one will be able to help me out of this downward spiral.
No one can glue the fragments of my heart back together.
No one can help my soul rebuild itself back to the strong willful part of
me that it once was.
I don't even know if I can help myself . . .

The Need To Heal

I curl up in a corner and hide my face.
Light fills the room, yet I do not wish to have it touch my skin,
My face,
My life.
For I am embarrassed to be seen.
I stare at my thigh . . .
Unwillingly I see his hand side up and down time after time.
I turn my head away and squint my eyes as I cringe.
Time after time I promise myself I will never let another soul take
advantage of me again.
A tear falls as I remember I made the same promise to myself years
before I was even touched by the disgusting monster.

I pull the tie out and let my hair fall upon my shoulders,
I use it as a shield to hide myself from the world.
I do not wish for the world to see my tears of pain,
I do not wish for the world to see how its stupidity has hurt me in a way
that
I will never be able to heal again.

I curse the soul that laid his hands upon me time after time,
I scream . . .
I curse . . .
I burn with the rage of a wild fire.
What right did he have that I did not?
I was violated, yet he walks through life as though he did nothing of the
sort.
He still holds his head high,
He still eyes the passing girl the same way he eyed my body,
As if a woman to him is nothing but an object at his disposal!
I ask myself . . .
What man would have dignity after committing such an offense?
Then I wonder what fool would let a man of this sort walk the streets
without a consequence in his belt?

I cry for hours on end,
I am hurt,
I am wounded,
I am in pain,
Yet I know no cure for what I feel.
I wonder will I ever forgive,
Forgive myself for letting such a humiliating event happen to someone
that could have stopped it?

The light sneaks through my hair and I am compelled to look,
and I see my future.
I see me years from now,
a grown woman,
happy,
With a beautiful smile on my face as I enjoy my life and what it has to
offer.
Once in a while I think back to the dreadful time that forever left a
gaping wound in my life.
I may think about it,
But it does not change the empowered woman I am.

I wonder when I will feel the enlightenment I feel
in this vision.
I feel as though a hand is rested on my should
and quietly a voice whispers,
"One day . . ."

Hope

The fire rages in the middle of the forest,
Water tries to extinguish it but it seems almost impossible.
It grows larger and larger, no one knows how long it will rage on.
The heat is so intense that the fire alone would lose its ability to strike fear into the souls of others.
The water fights and fights.
It tries to release the forest from the claws of pain.
The water digs deeper and deeper, trying so desperately to find the courage it desires.
But the fire grows and grows and grows . . .
Hope seems almost out of reach.
Somewhere inside, the water finds the strength that it needs to continue on.
It keeps fighting,
Slowly but surely,
The water wins,
The fire disappears leaving nothing but chaos and destruction.
It was a noble victory.

~ DEPRESSION ~

"The demon from hell that walks among us."

A Young Girl Cries in the Middle of the Night

A young girl cries in the middle of the night,
But no one hears.
She cries louder and louder,
Still no one comes to her aid.
She cries as the pain digs deeper and deeper into her soul.
Her heart aches with every beat.
Her self-esteem is falling apart.

She soon begins to wallow in her grief.
It isn't long until she's swimming in the tears that she's cried,
Her eyes are a midnight thunderstorm; rain pours without a second thought.
Her bed is the only place where she feels safe.
Her bed is what protects her from the harsh reality of life.

But as time goes on,
Even her bed isn't enough.
Her place of slumber is filled with the tears she has cried for her memories.
She spends hour after hour laying in bed,
Thinking.
She thinks about all that she cannot do and all she wishes she could change.
Her eyes once again begin to well up with tears,
Each tear has a meaning of its own . . .
Hate . . .
Embarrassment . . .
Love . . .
Guilt . . .
Failure . . .
Frustration . . .

Anger...
Sadness...
Uselessness...
Pity...
And *depression*...
She cries her heart out, but no one hears.

A spectator soon realizes what is happening.
He hears her cry for help,
But covers his ears.
He sees her sinking deeper and deeper into a bottomless pit,
But he turns away.
He hopes that one day she can find the strength,
To bring herself out of this rut.
Months pass,
Still she sinks deeper and deeper into a place where nothing can be heard,
And nothing can be felt,
Except for the pity and self hate she pours into herself.

The thought of reaching out never crosses her mind.
The only thought of help that she dreams of...
Is that maybe,
Just maybe,
Someone will not cover their ears,
And maybe someone will not turn away at the sight of her tears.
Maybe someone will reach out to her.

Months after months pass,
Still,
A young girl cries in the middle of the night
But no one hears.
No one knows of the pain and sorrow that pulls her farther and farther away.

Change

    I sit alone on the couch, thinking to myself. I watch the movement of people as they walk by. Each has different body language than the last. I blankly stare at the floor for moments on end, is this it? Is this what my life is? How can one call this 'living your life'? I sit alone, no one to my left and no one to my right.

    I stare at the couch that sits across from me. I wonder if it has had many people sitting on it thinking exactly what I am thinking. Where is my life going? I feel as though I am wasting this gift that God has given me. I feel as though He is, as I am, disappointed, in the course of my life. I have taken many paths. Many have not left me with a feeling of pride or honour. I am embarrassed about the way I live my life. I have not loved another, nor have I been loved. I have not had children, nor has anyone looked to me as a mother. Few know my name, even fewer know what goes on behind the mask. What have I done with my life that gives me the right to continue to live the way I do?

    I have not seen the world, my eyes gazing upon the wonders of the world is only a dream that I can imagine. I have not changed someone's life for the better, nor have I felt that anyone has impacted mine. If God has put me on this earth for a reason, when will I know what that reason is? Will I ever know what that reason is? I don't think anyone can change how I feel about my lifestyle. I don't know if I can even change how I view my lifestyle. My inner thoughts are different from anyone else's. I hide from the eyes of people and I expand my personal space much larger than the average person. I do not like people getting close, nor do I like the fact that some understand what I hide from the when even I don't understand. A lonely tear falls and I quickly wipe it away, I do not wish for those around me to see me when I am tearing myself apart inside.

    A young man sits on the couch that I have been watching for a few moments as I wallowed in my pit of self pity. There is something different about him, but I cannot put my finger on it. He does not have an evil heart, nor is his soul cold with devilish thoughts and feelings. He picks up a magazine and turns to a random page. I watch his movement as I wonder why he would not start at the beginning, such as the average person would. Again he flips through and lands on a random page. Finally, curiosity takes over and I have to ask him . . . why? His response makes me think, yet understand. "Why start at the beginning if you are not there? Why read the articles that talk only of misery in this world. Why not read the articles that shine light on the good events that happen?" I'm puzzled and slowly my mind digs to find the meaning of this, I come up blank . . . at least until I go back to the train of thought that I was on.

Then God gave me a thought that changes my life. Why focus on the bad when there is so much good? I run through all that is good and all that is great in my life and I smile. I smile a smile that I have not seen in so long. For the first time in a long time . . . I am happy.

Sickness

My heart is falling apart and I cannot stop it.
I am in pain, but I do not know how to relieve it.
I am sick, but there is no treatment and no cure.
My soul is melting, but I do not know why.
I can understand how I am feeling, but I cannot understand how I arrived at this place.
I am tired, but I cannot rest.
I pretend it does not effect me but it does.
Something is tearing me apart but I do not know what it is.
A ball sits in the pit of my stomach, but I do not know how to remove it.
I feel dizzy but I can stand tall or for just long enough that I can look as though everything is fine.
I feel a numbness all throughout my body.
yet I can still feel this pain.

Realization

I spent some time with you,
It was just me and you were just you.
We were not divided from the person that we actually are,
We were not the people that society has created for us,
We were ourselves.
I was the quiet, soft-souled person that I am.
You were the funny relaxed person that you are.
We talked and I didn't cower like a freshly embarrassed fool.
You didn't hold anything against me.
I felt as though we were like the people that we are, not the people that
we pretend to be.

As we talked a little more,
it was almost like having our armor was removed,
Leaving our inner selves unprotected to the dangers of the world.

I felt relieved as I realized that I showed you who I really was.
I smiled at all the embarrassing things I have done infront of your eyes,
because I know that you do not care.
I smiled as you laughed at my stupid childish jokes that were just created
on the spot.

Sentences that I didn't wish to think began to pop in my mind and off
the tip of my tongue.
Some I was embarrassed as I realized the meaning of their existence.
Some I had to laugh about because they were so exaggerated that no
one in their right mind would think of them.

You made me bare a grin that I had not seen in so long.
I finally remembered the feeling of true joy.
For the first time in a long time, I didn't feel miserable
I didn't feel depressed . . .
I felt a new feeling that I may or never may feel again.
But for a few moments,
I realized that there is still hope for me to beat this dark demon of
depression.

The Truth About Depression

Depression:
A vial word that makes oneself sink deep into a pit of evil.
Depression:
Causes oneself to think that no one loves them.
Depression:
A heartless state that will take over the lives of its victims.
Depression:
Makes oneself think that it will hurt too much to heal; making it harder to ask for help.
Depression:
A monster that is more crude and evil than the green jealous one.
Depression:
An emotion in one's life that causes them think they have nothing else for which to live.
Depression:
Pain that buries itself deeper and deeper into the heart and soul of a victim with its horrible black claws.
Depression:
A feeling in the pit of one's stomach as it slowly eats away at them.
Depression:
An emotion that is so easy to come across but extremely hard to leave in the dust of the past.
Depression:
A feeling that makes oneself think this may never go away until the day that it feels that it has tormented them enough and moves on to another victim.
Depression:
However anyone wishes to describe it, it will always be a creature of the dark that will rip holes in the life of its victim, piece by piece.

~ LIMITLESS FREEDOM ~

*"Music is the soul being heard,
Writing is the soul being read,
&
Dancing is the soul being watched."*

Can-Can

To the Music of Offenbach

She zips up her dress.
She's painted herself like a doll.
She slides her stockings on her legs with excitement boiling over inside.
Behind the curtains everyone runs around trying to look their best for the performance.

She and many other girls file out onto stage staring at the curtains and imagining them being
drawn back momentarily.
She closes her eyes;
The curtains are drawn and it's time to perform.
She glances at the audience just as the music starts.
She dances . . .
and dances . . .
and dances . . .
The smile on her face is priceless.
The feelings inside can only be felt when she dances on that stage in front of strangers.
Her eyes meet the eyes of men;
They fantasize
Her eyes meet the eyes of women;
They imagine being her.
Many eyes in the audience look her up and down.
They watch as her body moves in unison with the music.
She feels so alive as she dances her heart out on that stage.
The radiance that shines through her skin is what makes her feel that her life is worth living.
Her problems are transformed into energy.
Her energy is what makes the performance vibrant and full of life.
Her legs kick up into the air,
Higher . . .
and higher . . .

With every kick she feels better and better about everything that is not perfect.
Her dress spins round and round her body, drowning her tanned skin in a sea of burgundy.
She feels the feather that sits in the bun on the back of her head bouncing as if nodding in approval of her skills as a dancer.

The music stops . . .
Her heart feels uplifted now that it has expressed itself in the only way that feels natural.
Her soul glows with joy as she has finally fulfilled its needs.
At last . . .
She bows.

The Road

The road runs eastward;
I walk along it with my best friend.
As I walk, I breathe in and out
I can see my breath moving each and every way.
The trees are covered in snow from the snowfall the night before.
The road isn't plowed yet.
I pray that they don't plow it, for it looks gorgeous the way it is white,
With the grey sky above looking down on the heaven the good Lord has created for me.

As I walk down the road, I reflect on everything and anything,
Until I pull my mind off of the topic of my life, and I realize that this road isn't just a road.
As I walk forward, I move along the road of life.
The twists,
the turns,
the potholes
all resembling different obstacles in life.
As another road meets the road of life, I realize that I have a choice.
I can keep going in the direction I am or I can make a choice to follow a different path.

More choices come into the picture;
the untamed trails leading off the road resemble a surprising choice I could make.
I could keep moving in the direction I am or I can travel the trail few dare to.

Finally, I decide that it's time to turn around and go home.
It's almost like looking back on my past, seeing where I have been and where I came from.
Sometimes it's funny how looking back can give you a different outlook on the past.

With every step I take,
a new memory pours into my heart and soul
Some break my heart and some make it stronger.
Some make my soul wonder why I choose to remember things that hurt me
in ways that can't be explained.

My best friend wanders all over the road, re-smelling the smells she
had smelled on the way up and visiting
new smells.
Almost as if she doesn't know where she's heading in life,
and her plan is to just bounce around until she's happy with the path
she has chosen.
Time after time she pulls and tugs on the leash wrapped around my
blue mitten.
I realize that she's trying to pull away,
but I refuse to let go of her.
Every so often she pulls at a time I'm not paying attention
And she gets away,
Much like the people in life.
They try to pull away and sometimes,
When they try hard enough,
They succeed.
And sometimes, we get them back.

We move farther and farther into the past.
The bitter wind blows against my already frigid face,
as the cold feeling runs over my whole body . . .
I feel forgiven.
I feel as though the sins of my flesh have been pulled away.
I don't fear them, nor do I wonder if I'll ever meet them again.
Fate can only predict that,
And fate is the twin of the wind.
Every time it makes a decision, something different happens . . .
Good or Bad.

The Crossroad

I stand at a crossroad,
The two options I am given are to go right or to go left.
To the left is change . . . freedom . . . the life I have for so long wished to live.
To the right is the past flowing uncontrollably into the future.
To the right is everything being as it was:
No change . . . just lies . . . tears . . . and boredom.
To the left is the chance to be happy;
it's the chance to move on and to do all I have ever wished to do.
To the right is, in some ways, a slow, depressing suffocation.
The air I wish to breathe slowly being pulled away and,
I may not notice it today . . . or tomorrow . . . or a week from now, but one day I'll notice
and it'll be too late.
To go left means for once to not know all that is going to happen within the next day . . .
or a week from now . . . or a year from now.
To walk farther and farther away from the choice to go right means
to leave behind the boring life that has stolen my childhood and has crushed my will to have a life.
To go right means I will know how each day is played out.
I will know what it is like to be trapped for years and years and wish so dearly to be free of the
chains and ropes that tie me to this . . .
a life with no way of breaking free.
I look to the left; I see the sun.
It shines so brightly.
I smile as I feel the warm rays touch me,
Showing me that there is hope for someone that has felt like a prisoner for far too long.
I look to the right; I see darkness.

The shadows from the right touch me and I shudder.
I feel cold and alone, as though I am out of reach of anyone that I can see or hear.
I close my eyes; to go left would be spontaneous, exciting and like nothing I have ever done before.
To go right would mean being practical and making the choice they want me to make,
Not caring how it will effect me.
I open eyes.
A tear falls as I am unsure which way to choose.
A voice inside says,
"make your decision and be done with it."
I raise my head high and sadly smile as I make my choice . . . .

A Deer Hunter's Prayer

To all the dedicated hunters who rise early in hopes of winning that trophy

Oh Lord,
As I travel to my safe haven from the world around me,
Please
Guide me safely to and from and in between.
Protect me from all accidents and mistakes that could end in horror.

Lord,
As it is opening morning,
I beg, I plead, I ask . . .
Please let a buck walk blindly into my line of sight,
so I may show the wife my new greatest accomplishment.

God, Please prolong this day just a few hours more,
So I may enjoy the beautiful and wondrous nature that I almost
feel you have created just for me.
Please,
Just a little longer, just to feel real soil beneath my feet,
The soft rain against my skin.
Please let me live in this moment forever.

It is almost mid-week Lord,
And I fear the worst.
A tear slowly slid down Ted's cheek as he announced the beer was almost
gone!
Please Lord,
I am on my knees . . .
Keep the beer in good supply!

As I leave the camp yet again for another year,
My heart aches a bit as I smile and laugh at the memories we have shared in this short week.
I thank you God for this week of salvation and enjoyment.
I thank you for the gifts we have received,
But I have yet one more wish to ask . . .
Please Lord,
If nothing else,
Let me return again next year.

Amen

~ HANDLING LIFE ~

"It's time that we stop doubting ourselves in the face of an obstacle and embrace every moment and overcome every challenge."

Don't Worry, I'll be Fine

Don't worry, I'll be fine,
I know the end draws near as I see the tears emerge from your eyes.
I wish so dearly to reach out and wipe them away.
I watch you move around; sorrow hangs over your head like a dark cloud.
I lay motionless, wishing I could tell you in the simplest of ways . . .
Don't worry, I'll be fine.

I look back to the days we played and lived as it were eternity,
I see your smile and wish to see it once again,
just once,
just once more before I go.
I want to see that smile that says all that needs to be said,
I wish to see the smile that I have so long begged to see.
My heart breaks as your smile is buried deeper within the cloud as moments go by.
But all I see are tears, every one showing the love you have shown me time after time.
I pray to God that for once I could cry,
just once I could let tears flow and flow freely at that.
Just so that you may see that I have loved and cared for you the same way that you have loved and cared for me.
But . . . I am not blessed with such an honour,
Still I hope that my eyes,
Big and Brown
say to you . . .
Don't worry, I'll be fine.

As you sit on your bed wishing that in some way I may stay,
I wonder if you remember all our times together.
I wonder if you remember all the memories that we share between us.
My soul hopes you do,
For they are what makes these last few hours of my life Heaven on Earth.
I smile slightly as I reminisce of all our beloved memories that we have shared.
An invisible tear falls, not one of sorrow, as I realize that I am going to better place,
A place of no pain, no sorrow, and no broken hearts.
I just wish I could say . . .
Don't worry, I'll be fine.

I'm Watching Over You

As I'm watching over you,
I see the tears roll down,
Showing no mercy;
They are the beginning of the end.
My heart breaks,
And a tear from my eye falls as softly as a drop of rain,
I wonder why you all cry.
This is . . .
A time of sorrow but also a time to celebrate.
I wish to see smiles upon your faces as you remember all the wonderful memories,
that we have created together as a family.
I wish to see you all smile as you reminisce of all that made me smile and all that made me dance with pride and joy.

I see you are heartbroken as am I,
I realize, that we have said good-bye,
But we will meet again.
But for now . . .
remember . . .
I'm watching over you.

As time rolls on,
I will watch from between the clouds
And I promise . . .
I will not a miss a thing!
I will see my grandchildren and watch them grow,
I'll watch my daughters
and day after day I'll say,
"Those are my girls."
I'll watch my wife and every so often whisper to her,
"I'm watching over you."

I see you are heartbroken as am I,
I realize, that we have said good-bye,
But we will meet again.
But for now . . .
remember . . .
I'm watching over you!

Heartache

Why'd you have to leave,
Why'd you have to go?
I stand here with this heartache,
wondering if you know.

I'm here all alone
with this pain I feel inside,
I'm down on my knees,
Catching the tears I've cried.

I thought you were my angel,
Sent from above,
To help me spread my wings
and soar like a dove.

So . . .

Why'd you have to leave,
Why'd you have to go?
I'm still here with this heartache,
wondering if you know.

I've spent so many days
in my own room
watching the world go by
and waiting for my doom.

By as I lay here
Drowning in my tears,
I start to open my eyes
and face my fears

So . . .

I guess you had to leave,
I guess you have to go.
But I'm still here with this heartache
wondering if you know.

But do you ever think of
the pain I feel inside
and
the tears that you made me cry?

That's why you had to leave,
That's why you had to go.
I'm still here with this heartache,
wondering if you know.

I'm still all alone
With this pain I feel inside,
I'm still on my knees
Catching the tears that I've cried.

Friends Forever

Friends Forever
is what we will be,
from beginning to end
and for all of eternity.
Friends Forever
is what we will be.

In the beginning, no one knew of
what was about to be born.
As two young girls we smiled together,
we played together,
and we grew together
into the people we are today.

Friends Forever
is what we will be,
from beginning to end
and for all of eternity.
Friends Forever
is what we will be.

We laughed,
We cried,
We smiled,
We took to the bad together,
and lived the good together.
We were there when each other's hearts were shattered,
We were there on the most joyous occasions of each other's lives.
Now as we move apart . . .

Friends Forever
is what we will be,
from beginning to end
and for all of eternity.
Friends Forever
is what we will be.

Though we may not be close together,
A part of us will always be with the other.
Drying the tears that fall,
Holding them tight when a hug is all that's needed,
And making jokes when a good laugh will do.

Friendships don't always last the test of time,
Whether they be near or far.
But our friendship will grow stronger and stronger
with each passing day
Because we are . . .

Friends Forever

A Cancer Patient's Prayer

Dedicated to my Sister, Lori
May you be Strong & Brave!

Oh Please Lord,
Save me from this nightmare.
Each night I dream of what might be,
what could be,
and what is.
I open my eyes to escape the horrors that plague my mind, but yet
They are the truths I am faced with every day.
Every morning I awake and it's just like the last.
I see the smiles of my family,
Yet I know they are only there to hide their concerns and fears.
I know, because my smiles are what hides all that I feel.
I smile to show them I am strong,
but I feel so weak.
I hold my head high as I try to show that I am brave.
But behind closed doors, I tremble with fear and cry tears of pain.
What is a mother to do?
Do I show my children what I try so desperately to hide from myself?
Do I drop everything and cry alone so I may not feel the urge to cry in
front of them?
Do I ignore every little thought, emotion, and sharp pain and pretend
everything is as it was?
What is it that I am supposed to do?
There is so much I wish to do and see,
But where to start?
With this disease you have given me
Everything has changed so much,
My thoughts, my ideas, and more than I know,
More than anyone could imagine.
How my eyes view the world around me has changed,
How I experience every precious moment of every day has changed.
The anger within has made me hate You at times.

Every tear I watch my children hold back I curse You and the monster dwelling within.
But because of You, and this disease I pray to You:
For hope . . .
Hope that I will be healed and healthy once again.
For Strength . . .
So I may show the world that my spirit can not be broken.
For Courage . . .
So I may show the world I am not afraid.
For Willpower . . .
So I may have the will to continue fighting the battle that I did not wish to begin.
Oh God, If you can hear me . . .
Please help,
As I need you more than ever before
To give me Hope, Strength, Courage, and the Willpower to triumph over this demon from Hell!

~ *WAR* ~

*"We must realize that there are times when words will do
but we must also realize there are times when actions are required."*

Good-Bye

I wrapped my arms around him for what could be the last time.
Tears welled up in my blue eyes. I could not stop them.
He held me close, and tried to convince me that this would not be the last time
I would lay my eyes upon him.
I didn't know if he was lying, or if he truly believed his hopeful words.
I didn't want to let go of the love of my life.
But how could a *noble* man stay when a God forsaken war was destroying lives
on the other side of the world?
Why should my lover, and all the other men that stand beside him,
be faced with death and suffering everyday for God knows how long?

He was called to board the dreaded bus.
I felt my heart stiffen as I realized that he was going to leave me now.
My soul felt heavy, and as his warm touch left me, I felt it turn to stone.
I took one last blurry look at the man I may never see again,
He looked so handsome in the uniform that I cursed from the moment
I saw it.

We had one last kiss and he left me for the bus.
As he climbed the stairs he looked back at me and I didn't see a man . . .
I saw a soldier.
A soldier that was willing to laying his life on the line for a reason that
he nor I understood.

I waved good-bye as the wind softly dried the tears that signified the pain
I felt so deep inside.
This was it,
this was the good-bye I had been dreading for as long as the idea of
going to war crossed his mind.
So, what else is there to say other than . . .
Good-bye.

I AM

I am fearless and I am cunning.
I wonder what the land across the water looks like with the glow of the morning sun.
I hear the cheers and applause of crowds as I walk down the street with men on either side.
I see awards hanging over my left breast for all the bravery that I possess.
I want to be a hero and be acknowledged for my extravagant display of courage.
I am fearless and I am cunning.

I pretend not to notice the wounded that scream of the pain that the enemy has inflicted upon them.
I feel guilt ridden for the fact that all I can do is pull a trigger.
I touch the weapon that has taken so many lives, all of which I do not know.
I worry my sins will come back to haunt me and balance the universal scale that I have tipped.
I cry as I see death and false hope laying all around this battlefield yet . . .
I am fearless and I am cunning.

I understand men can be fools and believe problems can be solved with a few flying bullets and shrieking bombs.
I say there is a time for words and a time for actions.
I dream every night of the horrors of war that plague my memory.
I try not to acknowledge the *respect* and *honour* that is force-fed to me.
I hope one day these fools will realize that war is a murderer that cannot be imprisoned,
I know this because . . .
I am fearless and I am cunning.

I Pray

I sit in the trench, alone, dirty, and wet.
I cringe at the loud explosions in the distance as I cringe at the fear of them.
I die a little every time I hear a bomb explode or gun shot.
My soul is wounded and I don't know how much more it can take of this madness.
I watch the movement of the people around me.
All, if not many, are feeling exactly how I feel.

We are alone . . .
Anger is suppressed by the sounds and motions of the battlefield.
Depression cannot even show its face.
We wonder if we will feel true joy again.
I question if I will make it home,
And feel the warm touch of my lover.
I hope I will see my father and hear his words of pride.
I beg I will feel the love and joy my mother gives me.

I stand to my feet and look over the battlefield.
Scattered, bodies lay everywhere.
Some whole and some . . . I dare not describe.
The images are enough to scar me for the rest of my life.

I see a foreigner and I take aim with my gun,
Just as I am about to pull the trigger, I think . . .
This man has a story behind his face; he has a family that loves him.
He has a name; he is not just a nameless face,
As the lie I have been telling myself over and over has said.
For a moment I second guess ending the life of a man I do not even know.
The thought of my country slides into my wandering mind . . .

He falls to the ground,
I do not feel pride for what I have just done,
Nor do I hate myself for what I have just done.
Many times over this battlefield I have been left with the same feeling,
And many times I have prayed that the good Lord with forgive me for my sins . . .
I pray he shows mercy . . .
I pray . . .

The Letter Home

Dear Mom & Dad,   Date: April 15, 1917   Location: France

    Never have I been so sure that the world is coming to an end. I finally know for a fact that the apocalypse is no myth created to scare sinners. I see Hell all around me, I cannot escape it nor can I hide from it. If the world is to come to an end, this is how God intended.

    Last night as I sat in a trench clinging to my gun as if it would save me from all harm that is to come my way, I flared up with anger as I wished I was at home in my bed listening to the phonograph. Instead, I am sitting in mud listening to screams of pain and explosions that ended too many lives. I thought back to that day that I decided that I would go to war and *see* Europe. I remembered standing in line with a few of my friends. We talked as we waited to reach the front of the line, none of us had a full understanding of what we were really doing. As we signed our name, we literally signed our lives away. Our childhood memories would stay in our home town and we . . . the soldiers risking everything that God gave us would be traveling to a death trap halfway around the world. Now I have came to the realization that once every soldier returns to their quiet life back home . . . nothing will be the same.

    Once the anger passed, tears welled up in my eyes; I looked over the top and saw bodies laying everywhere. I wiped the tears away, for fear of being given the title *coward*. I knew that many of the bodies in no man's land were friends of mine, once dear to my heart. They were men with whom I trained. They were men with whom I spent my childhood. Now they lay in mud and blood. Dead! They had a need to prove to themselves that they had what it takes to live through such an event that will scar history for centuries to come. They were my friends, my kinsmen, now they lay dead and I can do nothing for their souls.

    I fear for myself everyday, every moment, every time I hear that whining sound of bullets flying out of the barrels of guns or bombs soaring through the air looking for the poor unfortunate soul that will be their victim. As I see my fellow soldiers wandering around in this new horrid lifestyle that consumes them body and soul, I see they are left with the same feelings that I am.

    I weep tears of remorse as I see so much death and destruction. I see buildings that once stood strong and gallant back when Kings and Queens ruled the land, now they lay in pieces. Bodies, oh how many lifeless bodies have I seen with my mortal eyes? Too many. The scenes flash before my eyes as I write about it as if I am witnessing every event that left men dead again, and again, and again. The first time I saw the corpse of a soldier that was once full of life and opportunity, I was scarred for life. I realized at that moment, that that could have been me laying there, that could have been me laying breathless with everything in my life that I had worked for going up in smoke without a second thought.

I myself, feel guilt ridden every time I pull the trigger of the rifle that my country has given me. How am I honouring my country, let alone myself, if I am breaking one of the ten commandments that God has gave us so we may live peaceful lives with good hearts and souls. I have murdered so many, and sometimes I am angered by the lack of control. Much like lemmings, we march to the slaughter. Cresting the ridge only to plunge into the abyss. I had no part in the creation of this death trap; that would suck the warmth from so many of my youthful brethren.

The day I was most guilt ridden was the bright summer day I came upon an innocent woman's tattered remains laying on the streets of a bombarded city. Her body was in pieces, ripped apart as though a heartless beast had killed her for its own amusement and left her to die in the street for the world to see its disgusting accomplishment. Then I wondered . . . how many innocent people have died because of me? How many innocent lives have been ripped apart because of this war? That was the first time in a long time that I dropped to my knees and prayed to God. I begged, I pleaded, and I asked for forgiveness of my sins. I asked him to protect all those that are innocent and have not taken part in the daily blood-shed of the war. I asked him to stop it . . . stop it all before there would be nothing left to destroy, nothing to kill. Just many sinners of the flesh.

Mom, Dad, I write you this letter to explain that I have come to my senses. I now know why you begged me to stay home instead of leaving and traveling into the hands of a murderer that cannot be stopped. I ask for your forgiveness. I ask that you forgive me for being another fool that enlisted for what he hoped would take him to Europe and show him the world. Instead, I was shown the part of the world that no one should see. I have learned so many lessons, some I wish I could erase from my memory and some I will cherish for the rest of my life and hopefully pass onto my children. Please, I beg, I plead, I ask for the forgiveness of my parents that have loved me for all my years and are now worrying day in and day out about the welfare of their son.

>This could be my last letter for awhile.
>Your loving son,
>
>Sandy

~ *YESTERDAY'S HISTORY* ~

"Today's events will be tomorrow's history."

The R.M.S Titanic

She sailed across the North Atlantic,
She lived by the name of the R.M.S Titanic,
Managing Director Mr. Bruce Ismay marveled at her and
repeatedly described her as gigantic.

Mr. Thomas Andrews also smiled proudly at his ship
As he believed that his Lady of the Sea was unsinkable.
16 compartments, 4 broken . . . she'd still live on.
At least until the unthinkable.

It was April 14th, when Titanic met her match,
She struck an iceberg at twenty to midnight.
The passengers shook, unsure what to make of the shutter.
They tried to keep calm trying not to have a fright.

The ship's crew scurried about, readying the lifeboats.
Captain E.J. Smith of White Star Line
gave the crew orders,
unfortunately knowing that not all would be fine.

The orchestra played on deck, attempting to calm the passengers,
As they slowly streamed out of their rooms,
The night was bitter, the moon did not show its face
as it knew that many would meet their doom.

The crew tried to hurry but time was slipping away.
The children cried for their fathers who stayed behind,
And the wives weeped tears as they hoped for the best.
But their lives would no longer be intertwined.

Those in lifeboats, watched as the ship's bow began to sink,
All wondering, "How could this be?"
The orchestra's heart began to ache as their strings began to sing
"Nearer my God to thee".

Women screamed as men pushed to ensure a spot,
Mr. Andrews stood in disbelief.
His ship would soon be at the bottom of the sea.
He now knew Titanic was as fragile as a leaf.

Mr. Ismay helped women and children into lifeboats,
Then at the last second he climbed aboard,
He sat still as the boat was lowered,
Quietly, he prayed to the Lord.

The bow began to disappear,
E.J. Smith knew this would be it
As the water touched his feet,
And yet, Titanic's lights were still lit.

Those hanging by the railing of the stern,
Were raised higher and higher into the air,
The second class minister gave passengers
his final words as they wondered if God gave a care.

Titanic's heart could no longer bare the pain.
A loud crashing sound rang all out.
The passengers in lifeboats had no idea,
what the noise was about.

The deck gave way, leaving the stern no choice but to fall.
Diving into the icy waters, the bow began to brake away,
As the stern once again began to rise,
all prayed that Titanic would see the next day.

The stern then bobbed upon the sea, those still aboard
gazed at the frigid water, fearing it's touch.
The hearts sank of those aboard the lifeboats
as they all knew they couldn't do much.

There was still hope as the stern stayed afloat.
Until the stern began to sink out of sight,
The survivors wept as they asked to see their loved ones again.
All wondering how this event in history could be called right.

As twenty past two came and went,
Titanic was gone.
Those floating in the water, begged the 16 boats to return.
Knowing that they would not see dawn.

The seven hundred in the lifeboats were ridden with guilt,
as they thought of the fifteen hundred freezing to their doom.
Officer Herald Moe took a single boat back,
But he only saved six and felt a horrid gloom.

At half past four, there was now hope for those that lived,
to tell the tale of Titanic. The Carpathia was their saving grace.
All seven hundred climbed aboard frozen by the North Atlantic wind,
All were unsure of what to make of the disastrous case.

Some lived through the shock of the century, but many more died.
Fingers were pointed and people were blamed but the fault should have been,
Given to the Fool because when he said,
"God himself could not sink this ship," it truly was a sin.

The Imprisonment of High Society

25 June 1908

Dear Journal,
    The dreaded date grows closer and closer. I am beginning to have nightmares as I walk to the altar of the church seeing the Priest and my dearly dreaded fiancé, Jonathon, smiling at me. They know I will forever be tortured as I would be bound to that monster disguised as a man. My mother, sitting so triumphantly in the pew nearest to the front, gleaming with pride, she knows that I have finally been defeated. Each night the dream occurs; I awake in a cold sweat on the brink of tears. I can still smell the horrid stench of those God forsaken flowers and the taste of wine burning my tongue as it unwilling slides down my throat. I turn away and hide the cringe from Jonathon. "How do you like it Elizabeth?" He asks even though he knows the answer. I turn my head and smile.
    "Just lovely my dear." I say just to please him, but that seems to be all that women of this time do, is strive to please the men in their life.

28 June 1908

Dear Journal,
    For the past couple days, my mother has been taking me to lessons so that I may learn how to serve my husband. I must know how to *properly* pour the tea for my in-laws. I must learn to not speak unless spoken to, and I must hold my tongue when I am compelled to speak my mind, which, I may add, is smiled upon by my mother as she hates the very words that may spill from my lips. The teacher, whom I call *The Wench*, has a peculiar way of teaching me these so-called lessons. In her left she holds ever so tightly a black rod, signifying that her heart has nothing more than evil within it. As a student, she believes that when I may prove the point that I am human and I make mistakes, that I may be whipped across the hands, the thighs, or where ever it may hurt most.
    As I was pouring the tea for her and my mother, once again I was whipped and, I wondered, "why must I learn the *proper way* to pour the tea? Why must I waste my life serving the bloody monster and his family of demons? They have two hands, ten digits, and at least half a brain; they

can pour their own God forsaken tea!" After the thoughts coursed through my mind, I stood up and threw the hot tea upon The Wench. "I am not a slave to you nor society. Jonathon can pour his own tea!" I hissed as I threw the tea pot on the carpeted floor and stormed out of the room. I came to the back door and slid out, hopefully unseen by my mother. I sat on the edge of a fountain that stood in the middle of the rose garden. I dipped my fingers into the cool water and began to daydream of all that I have dreamt about. I have dreamed of a life entirely different from the one I am trapped in now. I dream of all that could be good and all that could be better. Some days I imagine standing on the roof of the Queen's palace and saying all the things that I wish to speak and have longed to say for years and years. I imagine the crowds of people gathering in awe that a woman is speaking out; not silently hiding in the shadow of her husband. My favourite part of that fantasy is looking down and seeing my mother dying of humiliation as she knows I am going against all that she has been told by society and all in which she believes.

A grim smile came upon my face as I once again thought of death. As I evaluated my life once again, for possibly the millionth time, the thought of death, the thought of being free to roam where ever I may please, travel where ever I may wish in a form that cannot be controlled and cannot be contained. The feeling of freedom. I wondered what that would be like to not feel trapped and chained down fighting for a chance to live, only seeing the light of day growing dimmer and dimmer. My heart shatters as I know the day I say "I do," is the day the light will go out.

2 July 1908

Dear Journal,

The thought of death has become more frequent the past few days. Jonathon visited yesterday to show my mother and I his new firearm. Judging by the looks of it and from a description mentioned in a book I once read, it was a revolver. To annoy my future husband, I took the firearm by the grip and carefully examined it.

"A revolver, is it not?" I stated staring harshly into Jonathon's eyes. By the expression on his less than hansome face, I could tell he was more than surprised.

"How do you know that?" He hissed angrily as he ripped it out of my hand.

"Books can teach you many things dear Jonathon. You should try to pick one up and read it sometime, or do you need one of your servants to do that for you?" I slyly smiled and walked out of the room before my ears could be burned to a crisp by my mother.

I walked to my bed chambers, locked the door behind me, and sat on my bed. I closed my eyes, but I could smell a strong aroma of disgusting perfume. "My mother." I said as I ran for a tissue to blow the wicked stench from my nostrils. I walked to the closet, knowing with the least bit of doubt that she had hung the white wedding gown in it.

I gripped the cold handles as I knew the next sight I would see would be my wedding gown. The gown I would be wearing the day I would give up the last bit of freedom I had left. I closed my eyes and pulled the doors open. There it was. The gown that should be dyed the colour of the devil himself.

"Why must I be betrothed!" I screamed slamming the doors of the closet, "Why must I marry a man that is twice my age? My family has money of its own, I should not be traded around like a card." I fell to the ground and silently cried as I traced the embroidered pattern of my navy blue dress with my finger.

I shuttered. "I don't want to be married. Not to him. He does not respect me and he does not need my family's money. Why must I be auctioned off to the highest bidder?" I rose to my feet and walked to my mirror on the other side of the room. I sat and wiped the make-up off that has ran down my cheeks because of my tears of frustration. A picture of my mother sitting poshly on a stool and stares back at me, smiling because I gave in and wore the evil war paint that makes women believe they need it in order to be desired and called *beautiful.* I wiped it off, I wiped it all off! As the natural colour of my lips shined through, I smiled as I knew she could do nothing about it. I slammed the picture face down on the desk. "It's all her fault." I exclaimed looking into the mirror and seeing no need for make-up. Once again, my thoughts began to course through my mind, and my hate for her burned. My desire to be free of her chilling hands squeezing tighter and tighter by the day was growing as I knew it was her fault. It is her fault that she can not think with her own mind and must be told what she is to think.

"The firearm." said a little voice inside my head. I sat quiet for a few moments, staring into the abyss. The thought of death popped into my head. Maybe the only way to be free of this lifestyle that sucks one dry of the will to live is to be . . . dead?

3 July 1908

Dear Journal,

As I write to you, I am gazing out the window that oversees the rose garden. I find it too painful to sit as I was brutally abused the night before. Jonathon was in a short tempered mood. He, my mother, and I quietly ate dinner as a *family.* Jonathon looked up from his plate and was flabbergasted,

"Why aren't you wearing your make-up?" He asked as his fork hit the plate with a loud cling.

I politely patted my lips with my napkin as I felt I had finished my dinner. "I decided that there is no need for me to wear it."

"Elizabeth!" My mother scolded from the head of the dinner table.

"What's wrong with that? I have the right to make my own decisions, just as you think you have the right to arrange my marriage without consulting myself in the process."

"Elizabeth, you do not talk to your mother like that." Jonathon roared as though he was my father. I glared at him.

"My father was a far better man than you." I sneered rising from the table and pushing in my chair gracefully. I made my way to the doorway, but was stopped by a question sliding off Jonathon's lips.

"Why did you wash your face?" He asked slowly as he brought his hands to his chin and interlocked his fingers.

"Because I felt that there was no need to try to impress a monster and a witch." I stated proudly as I made my way to the back garden for a quiet stroll.

Cautiously, I opened the doors and shut them softly. The air was cold, but refreshing. The sound of my heels clicking against the hard pathway began to annoy me. When I heard the doors behind me open, I slipped them off and imagined burning the pointed things; I knew how much pain they had put in over the last many years.

"Elizabeth!" yelled Jonathon, I paid no attention to his voice, instead I imagined; I thought about death once again. By how he and my mother had reacted to not wearing a face plastered in powder and glue I realized even telling them to their face 'I do not want to marry the Devil!' would not have an impact. The only thing that could come from such an event could only result in another quick witted remark from myself and angry stares as they know I think too fast for them.

"ELIZABETH!" Jonathon angrily roared as he finally caught up to me and grabbed my arm harshly. He squeezed it as though he desperately wanted to tell me that I am below him and he is to be worshiped and served on hand and foot. I began to laugh in his face as I felt no intimidation from him. He slapped me out of frustration. I continued my laughter so he began to swing, hit, kick, and beat me. Still I did not bow down to that heathen; I stood my ground laughing as the blood from my wounds began to ooze out. I knew he had wished for so long to lay a hand on me just to teach me a lesson, just to make him feel as though he was **The All Powerful Jonathon.** Yet, by the impact of the blows which were becoming increasingly fiercer and fiercer, I soon realized that as I laughed and cackled he did not feel that the blows to my body were showing his superiority.

I shut my eyes. I knew that even the slightest glance of his face wrinkling up as he prepared for the next blow to my body would make the laughs and giggles slide out even faster and more uncontrolled.

Finally, once poor Jonathon was out of energy, he backed up gasping for air. I rolled my body over to face the house as I tried to calm myself. I opened my eyes and I died a little as I saw my mother standing by the window sill shaking her head in shame as she stared at me eye to eye. A fire from within began to burn and the anger was intense. I stood up and walked over to Jonathon. I grabbed the hair on top of his head, held his head high, and I swung. The moment my fist hit his cheek, oh what a glorious feeling to know I only angered him more by not bowing down to him and displeased my mother once again for being a free spirit that cannot be tamed . . . the feeling for myself was enlightening.

As I threw the door open, I startled my mother. The fear in her heart was even more evident as I marched up to her and looked her straight in the eye, "You are no less a monster than he!" I whispered. I then made my way to my chambers.

10 July 1908

Dear Journal,

Last night, I came to my decision. A decision I should have come to long ago. I spent my night flipping through your pages and reading what I have felt for the past three years. All which have been miserable but the past year has been the worst since the day I was told I was to marry Jonathon.

Since a week ago, a few more beatings have taken place and each time I have fought back . . . causing the next to be more brutal than the last. Forcing me to believe that one day he may loose control and kill me . . . but not if I beat him to it! I refuse to lose this battle . . .

I see only misery for the rest of my days if I were to marry him. I see only abuse, disputes and much more that should not be brought into a household. The only way I see happiness is if I were dead. Last night I decided that today is to be my last day on earth. I do not see this as being weak or incapable of handling the issues in my life; I see it as saving my future children from their father and their grandmother. I see it as being truly free . . .

* * *

Elizabeth closed her journal and slid it under her mattress. In someways, she felt relief, it was finally going to be over. All she had to do was pull Jonathon's firearm out from the bottom of her closet, load it, place the cold barrel against her temple, and pull the trigger. Elizabeth stood and walked to her closet, reaching past the white lace and grabbed the chocolate box in which she had placed the firearm. As she pulled her hand out from underneath the dress, she eyed it up and down and cursed the repulsived thing.

"Hell decorated in white lace and trim," she said as she grabbed the dress and ripped it from the hanger. "I only wish that my mother could have heard that!" Elizabeth sneered. She flipped the latch on the window and tossed the dress out. Landing on the ground, it looked as though it were a pile of snow. Elizabeth smiled and picked up the box once again and sat at the foot of her bed.

Elizabeth opened the box and there sat the silver revolver and three bullets. She opened the chamber and slid in the three bullets. She closed it quickly and took a deep breath. "Any last words Elizabeth?" She asked herself. "Yes . . . thank the Lord that I will be free of my mother and Jonathon." She smiled and pressed the circular mussel against her temple. She closed her eyes and inhaled deeply and held it.

"Elizabeth what is you're wedding . . . OH MY LORD ELIZABETH! NO!" Hollered Elizabeth's mother as she opened the door only to see her daughter sitting on her bed with a gun to her head. Elizabeth opened her eyes.

A loud bang rang inside the house. Jonathon jumped from his chair in the living room and ran up the stairs to Elizabeth's room as quickly as possible. As he entered the room he melted to the floor . . . there laid Elizabeth's mother with blood oozing from a bullet sized hole in the centre of her forehead and there sat Elizabeth on the bed

"Elizabeth . . . did you . . . ? But . . . how . . ." Jonathon could hardly catch his breath. He couldn't believe what laid there before his eyes.

"You drove me to it!" Elizabeth hissed and once again pulled the trigger. Jonathon dropped like a fly. Elizabeth collapsed on her bed, she smiled and slightly giggled, "I'm free," she whispered through the tears of joy.